Dedication

This American Sign Language book is dedicated to my brother Harold E. Farrar Jr, my grandmother Maggie James, my two new grandchildren Kassie Ruby Lynn Dalton, Caleb Asher Dalton. Additionally, to one of my Orientation to Deafness Insructor at OCC; Professor Margaret Yellin.

A is for Apple

B is for Banana

C is for Cup

D is for Dog

E is for Elephant

F is for Forest

G is for Giraffe

H is for Hat

I is for Ice

J is for Jacket

K is for Kite

L is for Light

M is for Manatee

N is for Nachos

O is for Octupus

P is for Pig

Q is for Quilt

R is for Rainbow

S is for Sand

T is for Tadpole

V is for Violin

W is for Waffles

X is for Xylophone

Y is for Yellow

Z is for Zebra

About the Author

Gale Dalton IS THE MOTHER OF SEVEN CHILDREN (SIX BOYS AND ONE GIRL) AND HAS 15 GRANDCHILDREN. She established two mentoring groups, Daughters of Destiny for young ladies and Brothers with a Purpose for young men.

Beginner ASL Language with the English Alphabet is her Fourth book; The first book is Beams from Heaven, a poetry compilation, and her second book is Fun with Colors en Español y Inglés. Her third book Fun with Shapes en Español Y Inglés. Learn more about Author Gale Dalton at:

www.galedalton.com

EXCITED

HUNGRY

SAD

GOODBYE

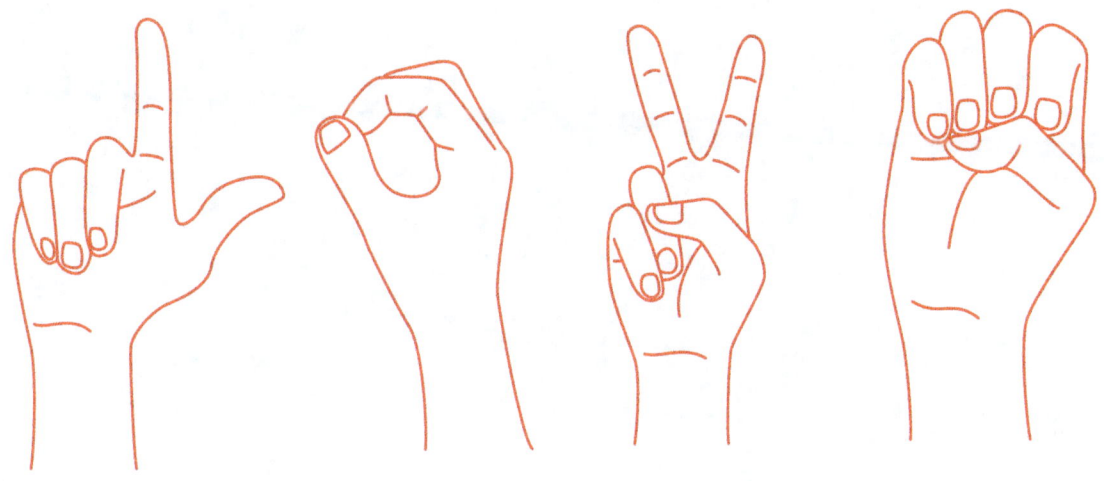